WORD PROCESSING

TABLES, CHARTS & GRAPHS

D0892376

ABOUT THIS BOOK

Tables, Charts & Graphs is an easy-to-follow guide to using Microsoft's word-processing program, Word, to produce professional-looking graphical presentations of data.

WORD'S FULLY FEATURED RANGE of commands and controls to create tables, charts, and graphs are clearly and simply described. This book is designed for users of Word with a basic understanding of opening documents, entering text, and saving the results. Word's features are presented in separate chapters to allow easy understanding of functions and how to carry them out.

Within each chapter, you'll find subsections that also deal with self-contained procedures. These build on previous explanations so your knowledge can be gradually developed through a logical sequence of actions.

The chapters and the subsections use a step-by-step approach. Virtually every step is accompanied by an illustration showing how your screen should look at each stage. If you work through the steps, you'll soon start feeling comfortable that you're learning and making progress.

The book contains several features to help you understand both what is

Word contains a wide range of tables, charts, and graphs that will meet any specifications.

happening on screen and what you need to do. A labeled Word window is included to show you where to find the important elements that are used in Word. This is followed by an illustration of the rows of buttons, or "toolbars," at the top of the screen, to help you find your way around these invaluable controls.

Command keys, such as ENTER and CTRL, are shown in these rectangles: Enter↵ and Ctrl, so that there's no confusion, for example, over whether you should press that key, or type the letters "ctrl". Cross-references are shown in the text as left- or right-hand page icons: ◁ and ▷. The page number and the reference are shown at the foot of the page.

In addition to the step-by-step sections, there are also boxes that describe and explain particular features of Word in detail, and tip boxes that provide alternative methods and shortcuts. Finally, at the back of the book, you will find a glossary explaining useful terms and a comprehensive index.

ESSENTIAL **DK** COMPUTERS

WORD PROCESSING

TABLES, CHARTS & GRAPHS

SUE ETHERINGTON

A Dorling Kindersley Book

Dorling Kindersley
LONDON, NEW YORK, DELHI, SYDNEY,
PARIS, MUNICH, JOHANNESBURG

Produced for Dorling Kindersley Limited by
Design Revolution, Queens Park Villa,
30 West Drive, Brighton, East Sussex BN2 2GE

EDITORIAL DIRECTOR Ian Whitelaw
SENIOR DESIGNER Andy Ashdown
PROJECT EDITOR John Watson
DESIGNER Paul Bowler

MANAGING EDITOR Sharon Lucas
SENIOR MANAGING ART EDITOR Derek Coombes
DTP DESIGNER Sonia Charbonnier
PRODUCTION CONTROLLER Wendy Penn

Published in Great Britain in 2000 by
Dorling Kindersley Limited,
9 Henrietta Street, London WC2E 8PS

2 4 6 8 10 9 7 5 3

A CIP catalog record for this book is available from the British Library.

ISBN 0-7513-0997-4

Color reproduced by First Impressions, London
Printed in Italy by Graphicom

For our complete
catalog visit
www.dk.com

CONTENTS

MICROSOFT WORD

Microsoft Word has been around for well over a decade and, with each new release, adds to its reputation as the world's leading word-processing program.

WHAT CAN WORD DO?

The features contained in Word make it one of the most flexible word-processing programs available. Word can be used to write anything from shopping lists to large publications that contain, in addition to the main text, illustrations and graphics, charts, tables and graphs, captions, headers and footers, cross references, footnotes, indexes, and glossaries – all of which are easily managed by Word. Word can check spelling and grammar, check text readability, search and replace text, import data, sort data, perform calculations, and provide templates for many types of documents from memos to Web pages. The comprehensive and versatile design, formatting, and layout options in Word make it ideal for desktop publishing on almost any scale. In short, there's very little that Word cannot do.

WHAT IS A WORD DOCUMENT?

In its simplest form, a Word document is a sequence of characters that exists in a computer's memory. Using Word, a document can be edited, added to, and given a variety of layouts. Once the document has been created, there are a large number of actions that can be carried out, such as saving, printing, or sending the document as an email.

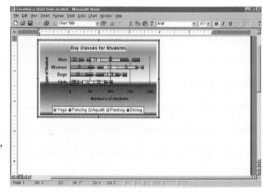

LAUNCHING WORD

Word launches just like any other program running in Windows. With the Windows desktop on screen, you can launch Word as the only program running, or you can run Word alongside other software to exchange data with other applications.

1 LAUNCHING BY THE START MENU

● Place the mouse cursor over the **Start** button on the Taskbar and click with the left mouse button.

● Move the cursor up the pop-up menu until **Programs** is highlighted. A submenu of programs appears to the right.

● Move the cursor down the menu to **Microsoft Word** and left-click again. (If Microsoft Word is missing from the Program menu, it may be under **Microsoft Office**.)

● The Microsoft Word window opens .

2 LAUNCHING BY A SHORTCUT

● You may already have a Word icon on screen, which is a shortcut to launching Word. If so, double-click on the icon.

● The Microsoft Word window opens .

THE WORD WINDOW

At first, Word's document window may look like a space shuttle computer display. However, you'll soon discover that similar commands and actions are neatly grouped together. This "like-with-like" layout helps you quickly understand where you should be looking on the window for what you want. Click and play while you read this.

THE WORD WINDOW

1 Title bar
2 Menu bar
Contains the main menus.
3 Standard toolbar
Buttons for frequent actions.
4 Formatting toolbar
Main layout options.
5 Tab selector
Clicking selects type of tab.
6 Left-indent buttons
Used to set left indents.
7 Ruler
Displays margins and tabs.
8 Right-indent button
Used to set right indent.
9 Insertion point
Shows where typing appears.
10 Text area
Area for document text.
11 Split box
Creates two text panes.
12 Scroll-up arrow
Moves up the document.
13 Scroll-bar box
Moves text up or down.
14 Vertical scroll bar
Used to move through text.

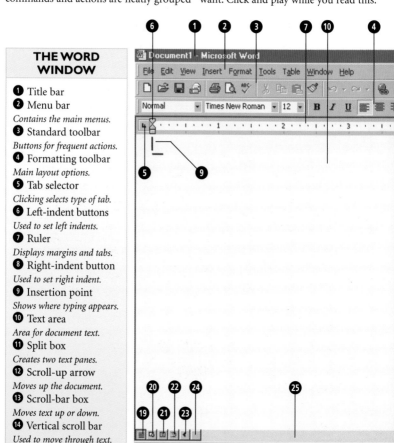

TOOLBAR LAYOUT

If Word doesn't show the Formatting toolbar below the Standard toolbar, first place the cursor over the Formatting toolbar "handle". When the four-headed arrow appears, (right), hold down the mouse button and "drag" the toolbar into position.

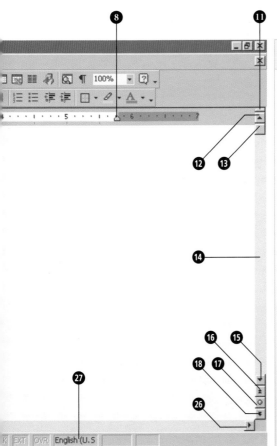

THE WORD WINDOW

⑮ Scroll-down arrow
Moves down the document.

⑯ Page-up button
Shows previous page of text.

⑰ Select browse object
Opens browse options menu.

⑱ Page-down button
Displays next page of text.

⑲ Normal view
Default document view.

⑳ Web layout view
Web-browser page view.

㉑ Page layout view
Printed-page view of text.

㉒ Outline view
Shows document's structure.

㉓ Left-scroll arrow
Shows the text to the left.

㉔ Scroll-bar box
Moves text horizontally.

㉕ Horizontal scroll bar
To view wide documents.

㉖ Right-scroll arrow
Shows the text to the right.

㉗ Language
Spelling, thesaurus, and proofing settings.

THE WORD TOOLBARS

Word provides a range of toolbars where numerous commands and actions are available. The principal toolbars are the Standard toolbar and the Formatting toolbar, which contain the most frequently used features of Word. There are also more than 20 other toolbars available for display. Click on **Tools** in the Menu bar, move the cursor down to **Customize,** and click the mouse button. The **Customize** dialog box opens. Click the **Toolbars** tab to view the variety of toolbars available.

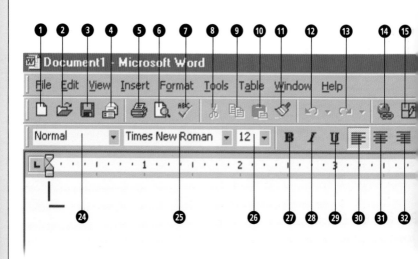

THE STANDARD TOOLBAR

1. New document
2. Open folder or file
3. Save
4. Email
5. Print
6. Print preview
7. Spelling and grammar
8. Cut
9. Copy text
10. Paste text
11. Format painter
12. Undo action(s)
13. Redo action(s)
14. Insert hyperlink
15. Tables and borders
16. Insert table
17. Insert Excel worksheet
18. Columns
19. Drawing toolbar
20. Document map
21. Show/hide formatting marks
22. Zoom view of text
23. Microsoft Word help

12 **Inserting Your First Table**

61 **Deleting a chart**

13 **Table insert button**

CUSTOMIZING A TOOLBAR

To add a Close button to a toolbar, click on **Tools** in the Menu bar and select **Customize**. Click on the **Commands** tab of the **Customize** dialog box. Scroll down the Commands menu to display the **Close** button. Place the cursor over the button, hold down the mouse button, drag the icon to the toolbar, and release the mouse button.

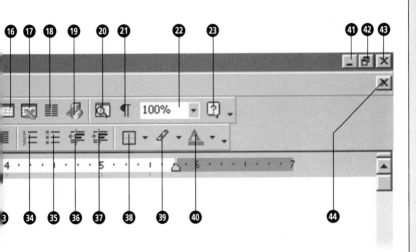

THE FORMATTING TOOLBAR

- ㉔ Style selector
- ㉕ Font selector
- ㉖ Font size selector
- ㉗ Bold
- ㉘ Italic
- ㉙ Underline
- ㉚ Left-aligned text
- ㉛ Centered text
- ㉜ Right-aligned text
- ㉝ Justified text
- ㉞ Numbered list
- ㉟ Bulleted list
- ㊱ Decrease indent
- ㊲ Increase indent
- ㊳ Outside border
- ㊴ Highlight color
- ㊵ Font color
- ㊶ Minimize Word
- ㊷ Restore Word
- ㊸ Close Word
- ㊹ Close document

12 Choice of Font

CREATING A TABLE

Using Microsoft Word, you can set up, edit, design, and format
a simple table easily. This chapter takes you through the steps
involved in creating and completing your first table.

INSERTING YOUR FIRST TABLE

Before you begin to create your first table,
click on **View** on the Menu bar and
choose **Print Layout** from the drop-down
menu. This view allows easy selection,
resizing of tables, and other options that
are not always available in Normal view.

1 INSERT TABLE
● Click on **Table** in the
Menu bar, move down to
Insert and select **Table**
from the submenu.

CHOICE OF FONT

Although the default font
in Microsoft Word 2000 is
Times New Roman 10 pt,
in the examples of tables
used in this section of the
book, the font used is
Arial 12 pt. This font
produces very readable
text both on-screen and
on the page. If your font
is not currently Arial,
open a new document
before you begin to insert
a table. Toward the left-
hand end of the
Formatting toolbar is the
Font selection box. Click
on the down arrow to the
right of the Font selection
box, and choose **Arial**
from the drop-down
menu. Click on the down
arrow to the right of the
Font size selection box
and click on **12 pt** from
the list of font sizes. Your
first table will now mirror
the examples in this book.

2 ROWS AND COLUMNS

● The **Insert Table** dialog box opens. In the **Table size** section of the box, enter the figure **6** in the **Number of columns** box, and enter the figure **5** in the **Number of rows** box.

● Click on **OK**. The table with the specified layout is inserted into the document.

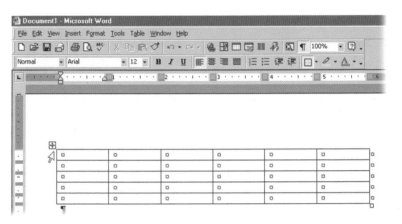

TABLE INSERT BUTTON

The Standard toolbar contains an **Insert Table** button. When you click on this button, a grid drops down representing columns and rows. The number of columns and rows is selected by holding down the mouse button and dragging the cursor over the grid until the required table size is shown. Release the mouse button to insert the table.

HOW TO WORK WITH TABLES

Before working with your table, a few terms and operations need to be explained. The parts of a table are explained here, as well as viewing a large table, selecting a whole table, row, or column, and moving around a table.

1 PARTS OF THE TABLE

● All tables consist of:
Cells – which contain data.
Rows – horizontal lines of cells.
Columns – vertical lines of cells.

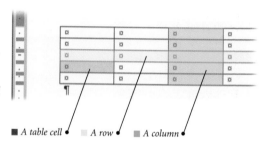

■ *A table cell* ●   *A row* ●   ■ *A column* ●

2 VIEWING THE TABLE

● If your table is larger than the screen, the table above or below the visible area can be viewed by clicking and dragging the vertical scroll bar. Use the horizontal scroll bar to view wide tables.

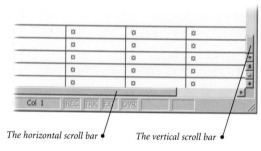

The horizontal scroll bar ●   *The vertical scroll bar* ●

3 SELECTING A WHOLE TABLE

● Position the cursor over the top left corner and the Table Move handle appears
● Place the cursor over it and the cursor changes to a four-way arrow. Click once to select the whole table.

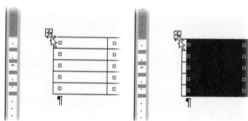

4 SELECTING TABLE ROWS

- Position the cursor to the left of the required row and click once to select the row.
- To select more than one row, click to the left of the first row, hold down the mouse button and drag over the required rows. Release the mouse button.

5 SELECTING TABLE COLUMNS

- Place the cursor just above the column until it becomes a black arrow.
- Click once and the column is selected.
- Select more than one column by holding down the mouse button when the black arrow appears and drag it across the columns.

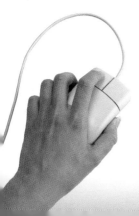

Moving around
To move from one cell to the cell to the right in a row press the Tab⇆ key. The ← and → keys move the cursor horizontally across cells, while the ↑ and ↓ keys move the cursor vertically. The Table Move handle, as its name suggests, is used to move a table anywhere within a document. It can also be used to select a whole table. The Table Resize handle at the bottom-right corner is clicked on and dragged to make a table larger or smaller.

INPUTTING TEXT

Having set up the basic table and understanding how to move around and make selections, the next step is to input the data. This section deals with column headings, manipulating them, entering data, and controlling how it's printed.

1 COLUMN HEADINGS

● If the insertion point is not in the first cell of the table, click in that cell.
● Enter the heading for the first column.
● Use the Tab⇆ key to move from cell to cell, or move the mouse cursor to the next cell, click with the left mouse button, and enter the column heading.

2 REPEATED HEADINGS

● When a table extends over two or more pages, you may want your table headings to be repeated at the top of each new page.
● Select the headings row and click on **Table** on the Menu bar.
● Click on **Heading Rows Repeat** in the drop-down menu. Your table headings are now repeated at the top of each new page.

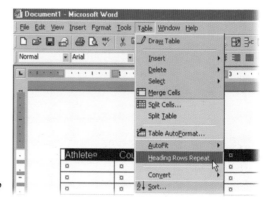

3 ENTERING DATA

- Now you can begin to enter the data.
- If the data does not fit on one line, Word increases the size of the row.

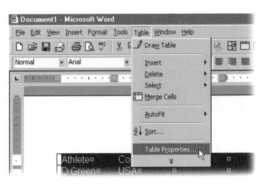

Athlete	Country	¤	¤
D·Green	USA	¤	¤
S· Belossovski	¤	¤	¤
¤	¤	¤	¤
¤	¤	¤	¤

4 KEEPING DATA TOGETHER

- When the data in a table occupies two or more rows, the data may split across two pages when printing. To prevent this, select the whole table ◻, click on **Table** in the Menu bar and select **Table Properties**.
- The **Table Properties** dialog box opens; click on the **Row** tab. If there is a check mark in the **Allow row to break across pages** check box, click on that box to clear it.
- Click on **OK** and all the data in the rows of the table will be kept together.

The completed decathlon table •

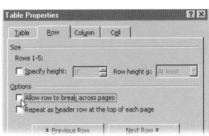

Athlete	Country	100 m	Shot put	High jump	Total
Athlete	Country	100 m	Shot put	High jump	Total
D Green	USA	799	854	888	2541
S Belossovski	Estonia	767	771	944	2482
W Harris	UK	852	728	887	2467
L Reyaud	France	856	648	803	2307

┌─┐
│14│ Selecting a
└─┘ whole table

SORTING DATA

Tables are most frequently used for organizing data, and you may have information in a table that needs to be sorted into alphabetical order. This is a simple task using the **Sort Ascending** or **Sort Descending** functions in Word.

1 SORTING ALPHABETICALLY

● Select the whole table to be sorted .
● Click on **Table** on the Menu bar and then on the **A-Z Sort** option.
● The **Sort** dialog box opens. In the **Sort by** section, pull down the menu and click on **Country**, which will be the basis for the sort.
● Click the **Ascending** radio button to create a list in alphabetical order.
● To prevent the row of headings from being included in the sort, click the **Header row** radio button to tell Word to exclude it from the sort.

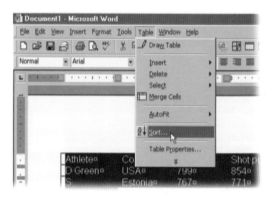

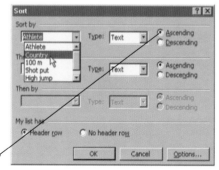

Ascending sort radio button ●

● Click on **OK** and the rows of the table are sorted into order according to the second column in the table, which lists the athletes' countries of origin.

● Click anywhere on the text area outside the table to deselect the table.

Athlete	Country	100 m	Shot put	High jump	Total	
S. Belossovski	Estonia	767	771	944	2482	
L. Reyaud	France	856	648	803	2307	
W. Harris	UK	852	728	887	2467	
D. Green	USA	799	854	888	2541	

¶

2 SORTING NUMERICALLY

● This table is ideal for sorting the results of a contest. Begin by selecting the Total column.

● Open the **Sort** dialog box (opposite), select **Total** in the **Sort by** box, and click the **Descending** radio button to produce a list with the highest number at the top.

● Click on **OK** and the entries are sorted in order of the points achieved.

100 m	Shot put	High jump	Total	
767	771	944	2482	
856	648	803	2307	
852	728	887	2467	
799	854	888	2541	

Athlete	Country	100 m	Shot put	High jump	Total	
D. Green	USA	799	854	888	2541	
S. Belossovski	Estonia	767	771	944	2482	
W. Harris	UK	852	728	887	2467	
L. Reyaud	France	856	648	803	2307	

¶

15 **Selecting table columns**

DESIGNING THE TABLE

Now you have set up your basic table, you can make changes to the appearance and layout. This section deals with options such as adding rows and columns, and changing the size of the table.

ADJUSTING COLUMNS AND ROWS

The number of columns and rows usually needs to be adjusted in any table. Columns may need to be added or deleted. Columns and rows may need to be of equal size, or they can be made only as wide or deep as the data requires.

1 ADDING COLUMNS

● To add another column to a table, select the column in the table next to where you want to add a column ⌐. In the example, the Country column has been selected because an extra column is to be added to the right to contain the details of another event.

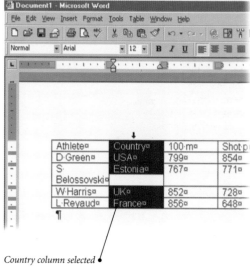

Country column selected ●

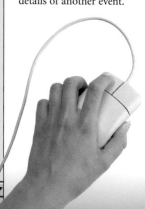

 Selecting table columns

15

● Click on **Table** on the Menu bar and click on **Insert** in the drop-down menu. In the submenu click on the **Columns to the Right** option.

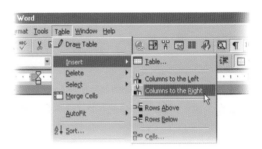

● An extra, blank, column is added to the table into which data can be inserted.

Athlete¤	Country¤	¤	100·m¤
D·Green¤	USA¤	¤	799¤
S·Belossovski¤	Estonia¤	¤	767¤
W·Harris¤	UK¤	¤	852¤
L·Reyaud¤	France¤	¤	856¤

Quick rows

To add a row at the bottom of the table, click in the last cell and press the `Tab↹` key. Alternatively, click outside to the right of the last cell of the table and press `Enter↵`.

Athlete¤	Country¤	Javelin¤	100·m¤
D·Green¤	USA¤	803¤	799¤
S·Belossovski¤	Estonia¤	600¤	767¤
W·Harris¤	UK¤	756¤	852¤
L·Reyaud¤	France¤	689¤	856¤

2 ADDING ROWS

● To add more rows to a table, select the row in the table next to where you wish to add an additional row . In the example, the last row in the table has been selected.

Athlete¤	Country¤	Javelin¤	100·m¤
D·Green¤	USA¤	803¤	799¤
S·Belossovski¤	Estonia¤	600¤	767¤
W·Harris¤	UK¤	756¤	852¤
L·Reyaud¤	France¤	689¤	856¤

15	Selecting table rows

● Click on the **Table** menu, followed by **Insert,** and then click on **Rows Below**.
● A new row is added to the foot of the table, which can be completed in the usual way.

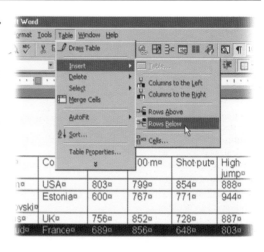

Athlete	Country	Javelin	100 m	Shot put	High jump	Total	
D Green	USA	803	799	854	888	3344	
S Belossovski	Estonia	600	767	771	944	3082	
W Harris	UK	756	852	728	887	3223	
L Reyaud	France	689	856	648	803	2996	

Athlete	Country	Javelin	100 m	Shot put	High jump	Total	
D Green	USA	803	799	854	888	3344	
S Belossovski	Estonia	600	767	771	944	3082	
W Harris	UK	756	852	728	887	3223	
L Reyaud	France	689	856	648	803	2996	
O Ngecki	Zambia	699	823	659	803	2984	

3 MAKING CELLS THE SAME SIZE

● The cells' sizes in the table may be different as a result of the different amounts of data contained in each cell.

● To make all the cells the same size, the width of the columns needs to be identical, as does the depth of the rows. Begin by selecting the whole table ⬜.

● Click on **Table** in the Menu bar and click on **AutoFit** in the drop-down menu. In the submenu that appears select **Distribute Rows Evenly**.

● Click on **Table** in the Menu bar again, select **Autofit**, and this time click on **Distribute Columns Evenly** in the submenu.

● The table cells are now all identical in size.

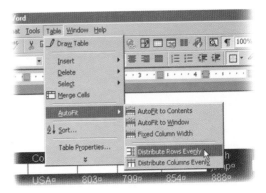

Athlete¤	Country¤	Javelin¤	100·m¤	Shot·put¤	High·jump¤	Total¤	¤
D·Green¤	USA¤	803¤	799¤	854¤	888¤	3344¤	¤
S·Belossovski¤	Estonia¤	600¤	767¤	771¤	944¤	3082¤	¤
W·Harris¤	UK¤	756¤	852¤	728¤	887¤	3223¤	¤
L·Reyaud¤	France¤	689¤	856¤	648¤	803¤	2996¤	¤
O·Ngecki¤	Zambia¤	699¤	823¤	659¤	803¤	2984¤	¤

¶

⬜ 14 Selecting a whole table

4 CHANGING THE COLUMN WIDTH

● You might wish to have columns in a table that have different widths. Word can do this automatically or you can do it manually.

● To have Word decide the column widths, begin by selecting the whole table □.

● Click on the **Table** menu, followed by **AutoFit** and then click on **AutoFit to Contents**. The table columns' widths are automatically adjusted.

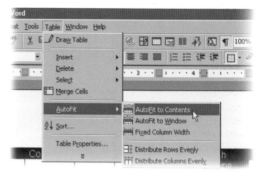

Athlete¤	Country¤	Javelin¤	100·m¤	Sh<
D·Green¤	USA¤	803¤	799¤	85<
S·Belossovski¤	Estonia¤	600¤	767¤	77
W·Harris¤	UK¤	756¤	852¤	72<
J·Revaud¤	France¤	689¤	856¤	64

CHANGING THE WIDTH MANUALLY

● Decide on the column divider to be moved and place the insertion point over it. The point changes to a vertical double line with two arrows pointing right and left.

● Hold down the mouse button and a dotted line appears down the screen.

● Drag to the right or left and release the mouse button when the column is the required width.

put¤	High·jump¤	Total¤
	888¤	3344¤
	944¤	3082¤

put¤	High·jump¤	Total¤
	888¤	3344¤
	944¤	3082¤

Country¤	Javelin¤	100·m¤	Shot·put¤	High·jump¤	Total¤	
USA¤	803¤	799¤	854¤	888¤	3344¤	
Estonia¤	600¤	767¤	771¤	944¤	3082¤	

☐ 14 Selecting a whole table

5 RESIZING USING THE RULER

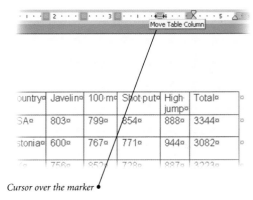

● Place the cursor over the small square grids on the ruler, known as *markers*. The cursor turns into a two-way arrow, and the **Move Table Column** ScreenTip is displayed beneath it.

Cursor over the marker ●

● Hold down the mouse button and a dotted line appears down the screen.

● You can now increase or decrease the width by dragging with the mouse. Release the mouse button when the column is the required width.

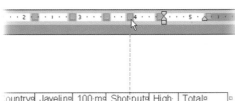

Displaying the width

To display the width of a column in units of measurement, hold down the [Alt] key as you click and drag the marker and the units are shown on the ruler.

6 CHANGING THE ROW HEIGHT

● Select the row line that you wish to change, and position the insertion point over it. The point changes to a horizontal double line with two vertical arrows.

| L·Reyaud¤ | France¤ | 689¤ | 856¤ | 648 |
| O·Ngecki¤ | Zambia¤ | 699¤ | 823¤ | 659 |

● Hold down the mouse button and a horizontal dotted line appears across the screen.

● Move the mouse up or down and the dotted line follows the cursor.

| L·Reyaud¤ | France¤ | 689¤ | 856¤ | 648 |
| O·Ngecki¤ | Zambia¤ | 699¤ | 823¤ | 659 |

● When the row is the correct height, release the mouse button.

| L·Reyaud¤ | France¤ | 689¤ | 856¤ | 648 |
| O·Ngecki¤ | Zambia¤ | 699¤ | 823¤ | 659 |

7 DELETING ROWS

● To delete a row, begin by selecting it.

● Now click on **Table** in the menu bar followed by **Delete** and select **Rows**.

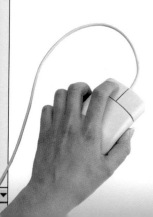

ent1 - Microsoft Word

View Insert Format Tools Table Window Help

Draw Table

Arial

Insert
Delete   Table
Select   Columns
Merge Cells   Rows
                Cells...
AutoFit

Sort...

Table Properties...

Athlete¤			00·m¤	Shot put¤	High jum
D·Green¤	USA¤	803¤	799¤	854¤	888
S·Belossovski¤	Estonia¤	600¤	767¤	771¤	944
W·Harris¤	UK¤	756¤	852¤	728¤	887
L·Reyaud¤	France¤	689¤	856¤	648¤	803

● The row is deleted and those above and below are closed up to fill the space.

Athlete¤	Country¤	Javelin¤	100·m¤	Shot put¤
D·Green¤	USA¤	803¤	799¤	854
S·Belossovski¤	Estonia¤	600¤	767¤	771
W·Harris¤	UK¤	756¤	852¤	728
O·Ngecki¤	Zambia¤	699¤	823¤	659

8 RE-SORTING THE TABLE

● Adding the Javelin points means the table needs re-sorting. Select the **Total** column and open the **Sort** dialog box 🖰.

● Click the **Header row** radio button and **Total** appears in the **Sort by** box.

● Click the Sort by Descending radio button and click on **OK**.

● The table is re-sorted in the order of points gained.

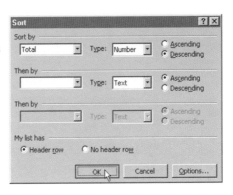

Athlete¤	Country¤	Javelin¤	100·m¤	Shot put¤	High jump¤	Total¤	¤
D·Green¤	USA¤	803¤	799¤	854¤	888¤	3344¤	¤
W·Harris¤	UK¤	756¤	852¤	728¤	887¤	3223¤	¤
S·Belossovski¤	Estonia¤	600¤	767¤	771¤	944¤	3082¤	¤
O·Ngecki¤	Zambia¤	699¤	823¤	659¤	803¤	2984¤	¤

18	**Sorting alphabetically**

FORMATTING THE TABLE

Once you have entered and organized the data in your table, the table itself can be formatted to emphasize different parts of the data and to improve the appearance of the table.

AUTOMATIC FORMATTING

Using Word's automatic formatting feature makes it easy to change the appearance of your table. Automatic formatting also helps you avoid "over-designing" the table, which can conceal data rather than making it more readable.

1 TABLE AUTOFORMAT

● Click anywhere in the table you wish to format.
● Click on **Table** in the Menu bar and select **Table AutoFormat** from the drop-down menu.

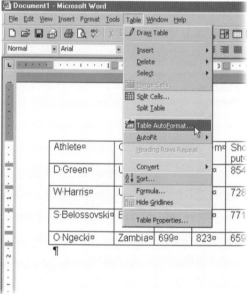

● The **Table AutoFormat** dialog box opens. The format selected by default is called **Simple 1**, and its appearance is shown in the **Preview** panel.

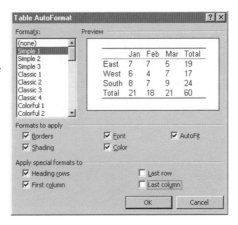

● There are a number of different styles of format, which you can scroll through and view to decide which style best suits your type of table.

● Click on the **Colorful 1** style of formatting and your table appears in that format.

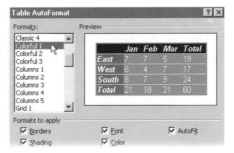

Athlete¤	Country¤	Javelin¤	100·m¤	Shot· put¤	High· jump¤	Total¤
D·Green¤	USA¤	803¤	799¤	854¤	888¤	3344¤
W·Harris¤	UK¤	756¤	852¤	728¤	887¤	3223¤
S·Belossovski¤	Estonia¤	600¤	767¤	771¤	944¤	3082¤
O·Ngecki¤	Zambia¤	699¤	823¤	659¤	803¤	2984¤

¶

2 AUTOFORMAT OPTIONS

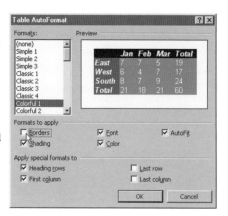

● The predesigned formats can be used either as they are presented or they can be customized. There are two sections of the **Table AutoFormat** dialog box in which customized settings can be selected, or excluded by clearing the relevant check box. In the **Formats to apply** section there are check boxes for various effects to be applied or cancelled. In the **Apply special formats to** section, different parts of the table can be either included or excluded from the formatting of the table.

● In the sample table shown, the borders have been excluded.

● If you decide not to use AutoFormat, open the **Table AutoFormat** dialog box  and in the **Formats** menu click on (**none**) and then click on **OK**. Your table is returned to its original format.

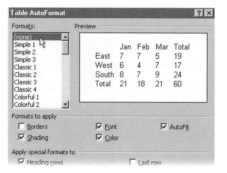

BORDERS AND LINES

To improve the appearance of a simple table, you may wish to give it a border, or gridlines within the table, or to shade the whole table with a combination of colors. These options can easily be applied by using the **Borders and Shading** feature.

1 CHOOSING THE LINES TO CHANGE

● Click within the table and click on **Format** in the Menu bar.

● Click on **Borders and Shading** in the menu to open the **Borders and Shading** dialog box.

● Click on the **Borders** tab if that part of the dialog box is not displayed. The **Settings** section at the left of the box shows the border options. When you click on an option, the **Preview** panel shows how the setting affects the text.

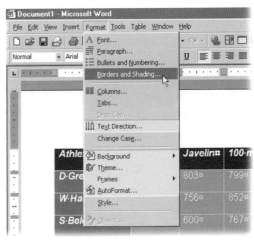

Box – *Only the outside of the table is given a border*

All – *The table and each cell has a border applied to it*

Grid – T*he outside has the chosen border style and the cell borders are made bold*

Custom – *This option allows you to decide where you wish to have borders. This is the option we are going to use, so click on* **Custom**

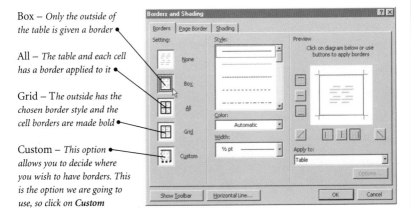

2 CHOOSING THE STYLE

● Click on the type of line you require by scrolling through the **Style** box.

● Click on the down arrow to the right of the **Color** text box and a palette of colors drops down.

● Select one of the colors, Plum has been selected in the example, and it appears in the **Color** preview bar.

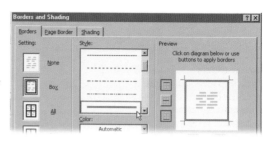

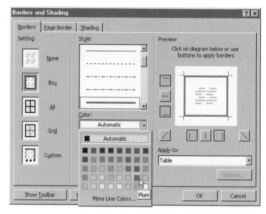

3 CHOOSING THE WIDTH

● Now choose the width of your line. (Note that not all lines are available in all widths. For example, the double wavy line is only available in the three-quarter point size.)

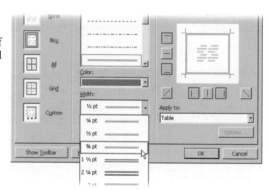

● By clicking on the boxes around the **Preview** panel (or on the diagram itself) you can decide where the lines are to appear.

● When you have selected a particular line for one part of the table, the same process can be used to select other lines for other areas of the table.

● When you have finished, click on **OK** and the lines are automatically applied to your table.

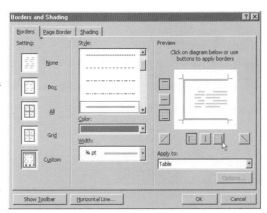

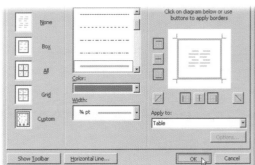

Athlete¤	Country¤	Javelin¤	100-m¤	Shot-put¤	High-jump¤	Total¤
D·Green¤	USA¤	803¤	799¤	854¤	888¤	3344¤
W·Harris¤	UK¤	756¤	852¤	728¤	887¤	3223¤
S·Belossovski¤	Estonia¤	600¤	767¤	771¤	944¤	3082¤
O·Ngecki¤	Zambia¤	699¤	823¤	659¤	803¤	2984¤

¶

CHARTS AND GRAPHS

Another way of presenting data visually is by using a chart or graph. Word enables you to choose from a wide range of charts, or you can create and save your own chart designs.

BASIC CHART TERMS

This chapter takes you through creating, editing, and formatting simple charts and graphs. Before we create our first chart, a few chart terms need to be explained. The most important terms are Datasheet, Axis, Plot Area, and Data Series.

BASIC TERMINOLOGY

DATASHEET
The datasheet is just like a table of information, but it is linked directly to a chart or graph. Using the datasheet you can input your chart data and see it automatically appear on your chart. Every chart and graph has an associated datasheet, which is displayed each time you double-click on your chart.

AXIS
An axis is a line that borders one side of a chart and provides a means to compare different values and categories. In our "Student Classes" example, which is used later in this chapter, the vertical axis, otherwise called the Value (Y) axis, shows the numbers of students. The horizontal axis of the graph, known as the Category (X) axis, shows the types of students, that is, girls, boys, women, and men.

PLOT AREA
As the name suggests, this is the area of the chart where the actual data is plotted; the location of the plot area depends on the type of chart chosen. The examples in this chapter show plot areas where columns and tubes illustrate the graphs.

DATA SERIES
This is a group of related points in a chart that originates from the rows and columns held on the datasheet. It is easy to see a data series because each one has a unique color or pattern on the chart or graph. In our Student Classes example, we have four data series – one for each category of girls, boys, women, and men.

A CHART FROM A WORD TABLE

Here we convert the data held in the earlier table into a chart. Microsoft Graph 2000 only converts tables to charts where there is one heading row and only the first column is text. All of the other rows and columns must contain numbers.

1 CONVERTING THE TABLE

- Open the document containing the table you wish to convert to a chart.
- As only the first column can contain text, delete the Country column by selecting it, selecting **Delete** from the **Table** menu, and selecting **Columns** from the submenu.
- Now select the whole table ⌂.
- Click on the **Insert** menu and then select **Object**.

Athlete	Javelin	100·m	Shot·put	High·jump
D·Green	803	799	854	888
W·Harris	756	852	728	887
S·Belossovski	600	767	771	944
O·Ngecki	699	823	659	803

Existing data

Word 2000 allows you to convert existing data, held in tables, to a chart or graph; or you can set up a chart from scratch in just a few simple steps. You can also import data from other programs such as Microsoft Excel.

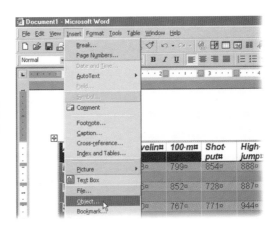

14 **Selecting a whole table**

● The **Object** dialog box opens. If necessary, click on the **Create New** tab at the top of the dialog box to view its options.

● Scroll down through the options, click on **Microsoft Graph 2000 Chart**, and click on OK.

● Now there are two new panels on the screen – a datasheet and a column graph, both containing the data held in the table.

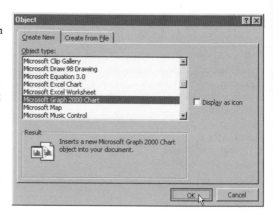

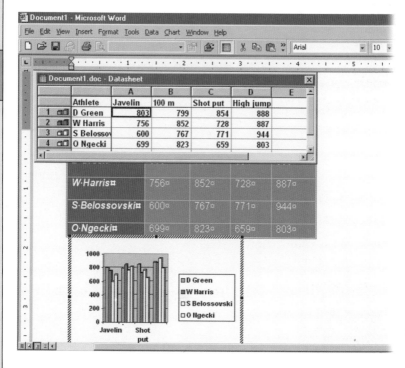

2 POSITIONING THE CHART

● The datasheet and the table occupy most of the visible area, making it difficult to move the chart anywhere. Remove them by first clicking on the **View Datasheet** icon on the Standard toolbar (or on **x** at the top right-hand corner of the datasheet window) to remove the datasheet from the screen.

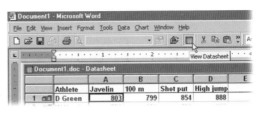

	A	B	C	D	E
	Athlete	Javelin	100 m	Shot put	High jump
1	D Green	803	799	854	888

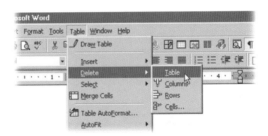

Athlete¤	Javelin¤	100·m¤	Shot· put¤	High· jump¤
D·Green¤	803¤	799¤	854¤	888¤
W·Harris¤	756¤	852¤	728¤	887¤
S·Belossovski¤	600¤	767¤	771¤	944¤
O·Ngecki¤	699¤	823¤	659¤	803¤

● Now select the whole table and delete it by clicking on the **Table** menu followed by **Delete** and then **Table**.

● The chart automatically moves to the position occupied by the table.

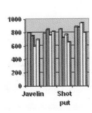

3 MOVING THE CHART

● If you wish to move the chart within the existing text on the page (which need only be paragraph marks), first click on the chart to select it.

● Hold down the mouse button and a small copy box appears below the mouse cursor.

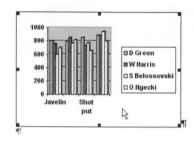

● Drag the cursor to the new location and release the mouse button.

● To move the chart across the page to the right, press the [Tab⇆] key.

● To relocate the chart back across the page to the left, hold down the [⇧ Shift] key and press the [Tab⇆] key.

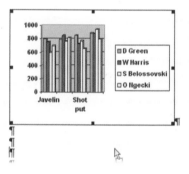

Cut and paste charts

If you wish to move a chart across several pages in a document, cut and paste is quicker than manually dragging the chart. Click on the chart to select it, click on **Edit** in the Menu bar and select **Cut** from the drop-down menu; the chart is placed on the clipboard. Move the insertion point to the new position for the chart and click on **Paste** in the **Edit** menu.

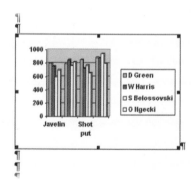

4 DIFFERENT CHARTS

The standard columns chart does not show the data in the table very clearly, and a different chart can be selected.

● Double-click on the chart. The word **Chart** appears on the Menu bar and the datasheet reappears. The chart now has a thicker border showing that it can now be edited and is not simply selected as before.

● As it's not necessary to display the datasheet for selecting a chart type, close it by clicking on the **View Datasheet** icon on the Standard toolbar or click on the **x** button on the datasheet.

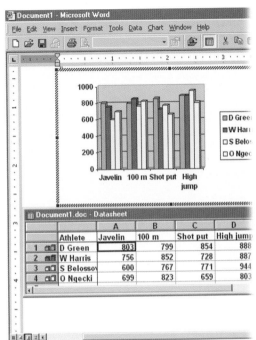

Click to close the datasheet ●

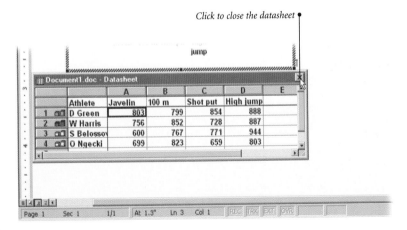

● Click on **Chart** on the Menu bar, followed by **Chart Type**.

● The **Chart Type** dialog box opens. If necessary, click on the **Standard Types** tab at the top of the dialog box. **Column** is highlighted in the **Chart Type** menu because it is the default chart type, which is why the table was first converted into a chart with columns.

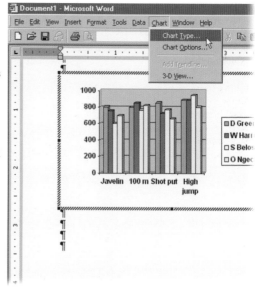

Column selected as the default chart type

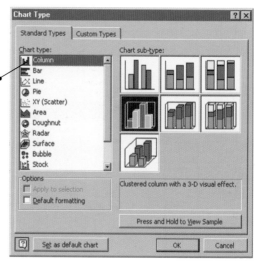

● Click on the **Cone** chart
option on the left and
select one of the sub-types
on the right.

● Click on the **Press and
Hold to View Sample**
button at the foot of the
window and hold down the
mouse button. The data is
shown in the chart format
that you have selected.

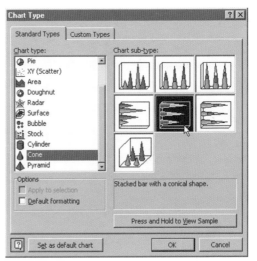

Tip
If the chart seems to
be missing some text
or data, it could be
because it needs to be
enlarged △.

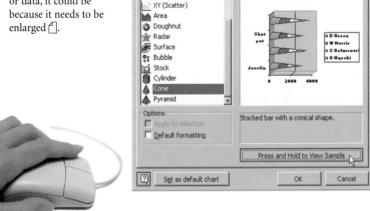

△ **Resizing**
46 the chart

5 CUSTOM CHARTS

● If none of the **Standard Types** of charts seems to display the data as you require, you can investigate the **Custom Types** on the next tab in the dialog box.

● Click on the **Custom Types** tab at the top of the dialog box.

● Scroll through the options available on the left of the dialog box. With these charts, the table data is automatically displayed in the **Sample** panel.

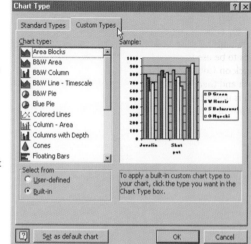

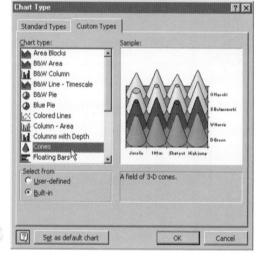

● The **Columns with Depth** option appears to show the table data more clearly, and this is the one that is to be used.

● Click on **Columns with Depth** and then **OK**. The chart is now showing the data in this type.

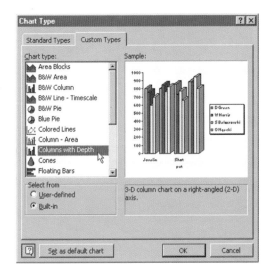

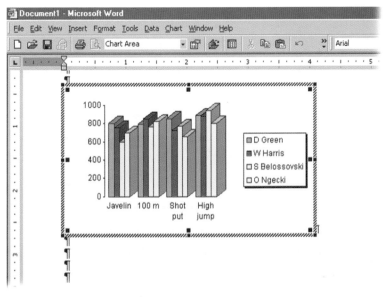

CREATING A CHART FROM SCRATCH

If you want to create a chart from scratch and enter data not held anywhere in the computer, you can do this by using the **Microsoft Graph 2000 Chart**. The program provides a sample chart and datasheet containing dummy information to help show you where you can enter your own column headings, rows, and data. This part of the book also covers some of the basic editing that you can do.

1 GETTING THE SAMPLE CHART

● Click in the document where you wish to position your chart.
● Click on the **Insert** menu and then on **Object**.

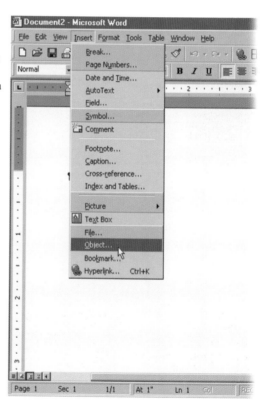

Choosing the view
If you want to be able to switch between the chart and datasheet without hiding the datasheet, just click on the chart or datasheet and both remain visible. If the datasheet is not visible, just click on the **View Datasheet** icon on the Standard toolbar. You can also click this icon to remove the datasheet from the screen when necessary.

● The **Object** dialog box opens. If necessary, click on the **Create New** tab.

● Scroll down the **Object type** menu and click on **Microsoft Graph 2000 Chart** and click on **OK**.

● Two new windows open on screen – a datasheet and a column graph, both containing sample data.

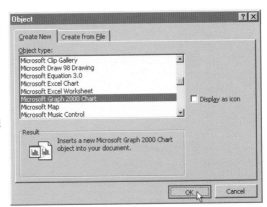

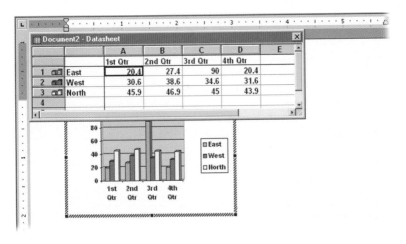

2 ENTERING DATA

● On the datasheet, click on the first column heading and enter the heading.

		A	B	C	D
		Girls	2nd Qtr	3rd Qtr	4th Qtr
1	East	20.4	27.4	90	20.4
2	West	30.6	38.6	34.6	31.6
3	North	45.9	46.9	45	43.9
4					

● Continue to add the information into the cells of the datasheet.

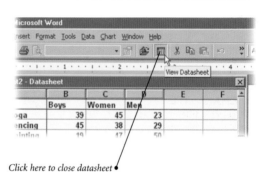

3 RESIZING THE CHART

● Currently the chart is too small to see all the data.
● Close the datasheet by clicking on the **View Datasheet** button.
● Place the mouse cursor over the right handle, hold down the mouse button, and drag the edge of the chart to the right.

Click here to close datasheet

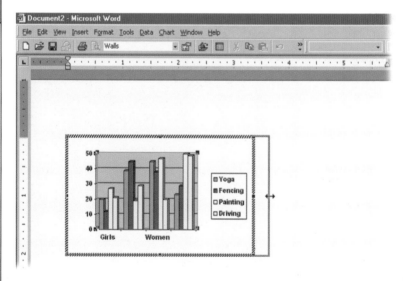

● When the chart is large enough to display all the information, release the mouse button and click off the chart to see the effect.

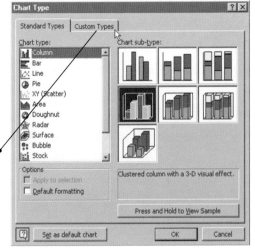

4 A DIFFERENT CHART TYPE

● To select a different chart type, first double-click on the chart and close the datasheet in the usual way if it appears.

● Click on **Chart** in the Menu bar and from the list select **Chart Type**.

● The **Chart Type** dialog box opens. Click on the **Custom Types** tab.

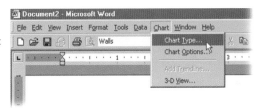

The Custom Types tab

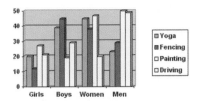

5 SELECTING A CHART TYPE

● Select the chart type that best suits your data ⌐. The chart chosen here is **Tubes** from the menu.

● Click on **OK** when you are satisfied with the type of chart chosen.

Choosing Tubes from the list of chart types

Moving the datasheet

Sometimes you might want to move the datasheet out of the way so that you can see the chart and the datasheet at the same time. Place the mouse cursor over the Title bar of the datasheet – the blue band at the top – and hold down the mouse button. Drag the datasheet to its new location and release the mouse button.

● Your chart is automatically displayed in the new format.

● If you want to change the data in your graph, double-click on the graph, click on the **View Datasheet** button if the datasheet does not appear, and amend the data as described above.

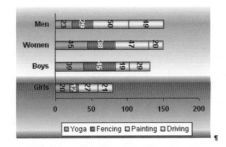

6 CHOOSING CHART OPTIONS

● Now that you have set up the basic chart or graph, you may wish to add a title to the chart and have text against each of the axes. The Microsoft Graph 2000 Chart program contains standard options that allow you to add further details to your chart or graph.

● If **Chart** is not already displayed on the Menu bar, double-click on the chart.

● Click on **Chart** on the Menu bar followed by **Chart Options**.

● The **Chart Options** dialog box opens.

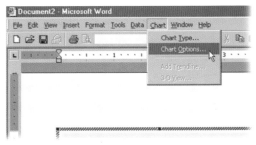

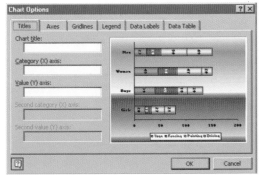

7 ENTERING TITLES

● Click on the **Titles** tab if it is not displayed, and in the first text box named **Chart title** enter a title for the chart, for example, **Student Classes**.

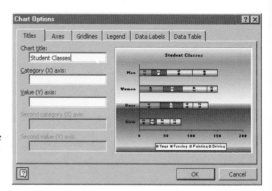

● Click in the next box, **Category (X) axis**. The title **Student Classes** appears at the top of the graph image at right.

● Enter the text for the **Category (X) axis**, for example **Student Type**.

● The X-axis is always along the *logical* bottom of the graph – in this case on the left side of the graph at the end of the tubes.

● Click on the **Value (Y) axis** text box and enter **Numbers of Students**.

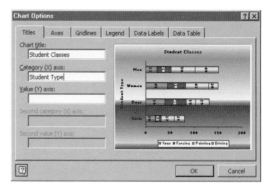

Y-axis label ●

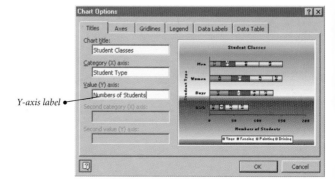

● If you wish to make any changes to the text, just highlight the text in the box and key in the new text. Let's change the X-axis text to **Type of Student**.

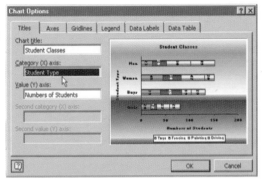

Tip
If at any time you press the Enter↵ key by mistake before completing all of the options, don't worry. Just double-click on the chart and continue as described above.

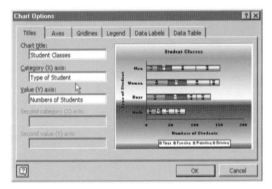

8 CUSTOMIZING THE AXES

● There are a number of options available with which you can manipulate the axes.
● Begin by clicking on the **Axes** tab.

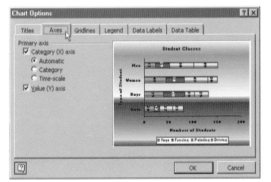

● The **Primary Axis, Category (X) axis** is normally checked. In the example, it details the categories of Girls, Boys, Women, and Men. If you click the **Category (X)** box off, the categories do not appear on your graph.

● Similarly, the **Value (Y) axis** may also be clicked off. In our example, it is showing the total number of students by type.

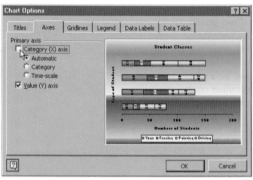

Rules of axes

When designing a chart, the conventions that are usually followed are that the Y-axis is the value axis along which data values are shown, and the X-axis shows the categories to which the data values apply.

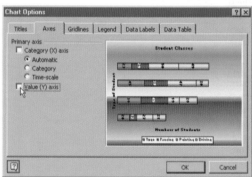

9 ADDING GRIDLINES

● Gridlines can make your chart more readable. To access them, click on the **Gridlines** tab.

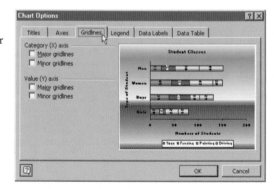

● There are **Major** and **Minor gridlines** available for both the Category (X) axis and Value (Y) axis.

● On this occasion, let's just leave on the **Major gridlines** on the Value (Y) axis.

● Click on **OK** to close the **Chart Options** box and click off the chart to see the effects of the gridlines.

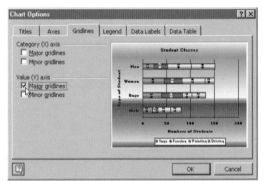

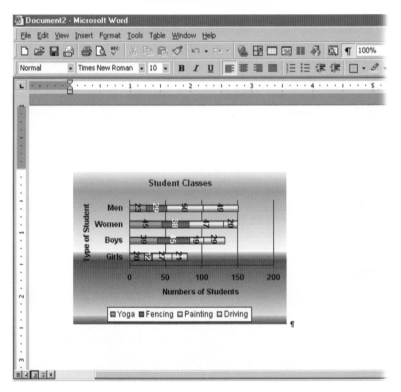

EDITING THE CHART

This chapter covers manipulating data in the datasheet which is then reflected in the chart. You can also add and delete columns and rows of data, as well as editing text on the chart.

ADDING ROWS

1 LOCATION OF THE NEW ROW

● If you need to add data to a chart, you might need to add rows for new data.

● Double-click on the chart if the **Chart** menu options are not already available in the Menu bar.

● Click on the **View Datasheet** icon on the Menu bar if the datasheet is not on the screen.

● Hold the mouse arrow over the row heading until it turns into a white cross.

● Click on the row heading below where you wish the new row to be inserted.

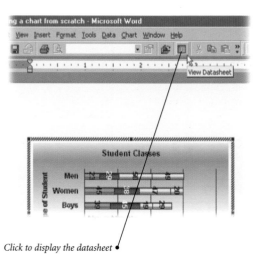

Click to display the datasheet ●

2 ADDING DATA TO THE NEW ROW

● Click on **Insert** on the Menu bar, and then **Cells**.
● A new row is inserted into the datasheet and you can now fill the row with your additional data. The data is immediately shown on the chart.

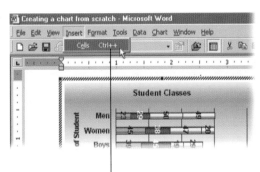

This option adds new cells ●

Adding columns

You can add columns to the datasheet by clicking on the column heading to the right of where you want a new column. Click on **Insert** in the Menu bar and then on **Cells**. The new column appears in the datasheet.

		A	B	C	D
		Girls	Boys	Women	Men
1	Yoga	20	39	45	23
2	Fencing	12	45	38	29
3	Aquafit	26	10	34	21
4	Painting	27	19	47	50
5	Driving	21	29	20	49
6					

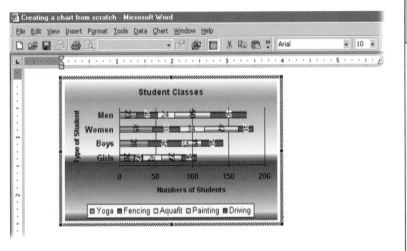

EDITING THE CHART AND TEXT

You might want to alter parts of the chart, such as the title, or the Value Y and Category X axis labels, without having to use the Microsoft Graph 2000 Chart program. It is possible to do this by working directly on the chart itself.

1 SELECT THE TEXT TO BE CHANGED

- Double-click on the chart to select it. If the datasheet appears, close it in the usual way.
- Hold the mouse cursor over the title of the chart and the words **Chart Title** are displayed.

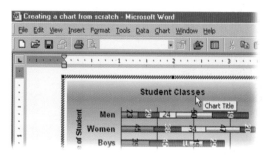

- Click on the chart title, which will now be enclosed inside a text box
- Enter the new title.
- Press the [Esc] key twice.
- The chart now shows the new title.

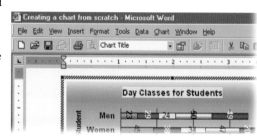

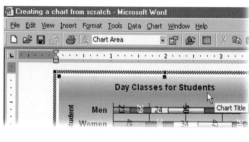

2 SELECTING OTHER CHART ITEMS

● You can select any part of the chart by using the **Chart Objects** box below the Menu bar at the top of the screen. Let's just look at the Plot Area – the background of the chart – and change the Chart Type.

● Double-click on the chart and the chart menu bar is displayed.

● Click on the black arrow to the right of the **Chart Objects** box and the list of chart objects is displayed.

● Click on the item you wish to see on the chart. Let's choose the **Plot Area** of the chart.

● Note that the Plot Area now has a border around it.

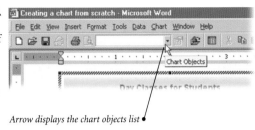

Arrow displays the chart objects list ●

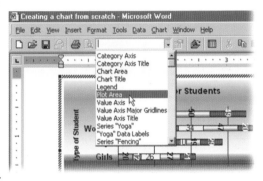

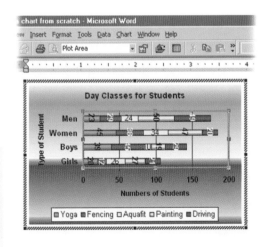

Tip
To revert to an original chart type, click on **Edit** on the Menu bar and select **Undo Chart Type** from the list of actions.

3 CHANGING THE CHART TYPE

● Double-click on the chart and click on **Chart** on the Menu bar.

● Select **Chart Type** to open the **Chart** dialog box.

● Scroll through the **Chart Type** menu and select a different style of chart. **Column - Area** is the type of chart selected here.

● Click on **OK** and the data is now plotted in a different chart type.

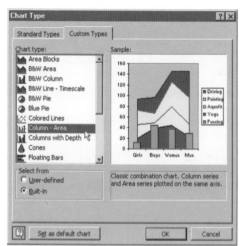

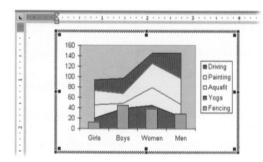

4 SAVING FOR FUTURE USE

● Later in the book (page 62), we customize the appearance of a chart using this chart type from the **Columns** options. If you wish, you can change your chart to this type and save it for later use.

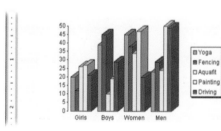

DELETING DATA AND DELETING CHARTS

Your chart may contain data that is no longer relevant. A quick way to delete data from a chart is to delete it from the datasheet. This section shows you how to delete data by using this method, and finally shows you how to delete a chart.

1 DELETING DATA

● Double-click on the chart if the **Chart** option is not displayed on the Menu bar.

● Click on the **View Datasheet** icon on the Standard toolbar so that the datasheet is again shown on screen below the chart.

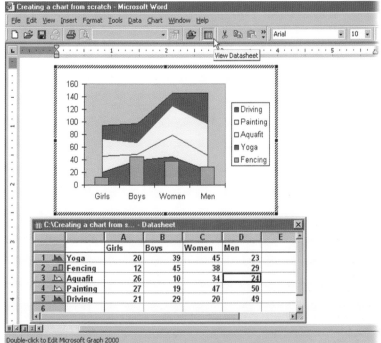

2 SELECTING AND DELETING DATA

● Position the cursor over a lettered column heading until the cursor turns into a white cross.

● Hold down the mouse button and drag the mouse to the left (or right) to highlight the columns to be deleted and release the mouse button.

● Click on **Edit** on the Menu bar and select **Delete**.

● The highlighted columns are now deleted from the datasheet and the chart is redrawn accordingly.

● Similarly, you can click on row headings and carry out the same steps to delete rows of data from a datasheet and the chart.

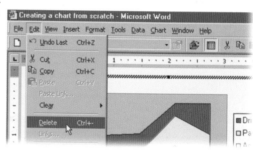

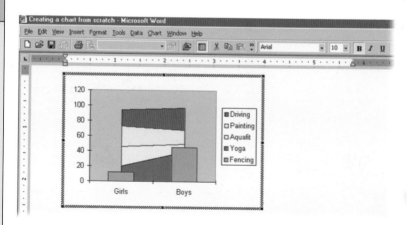

3 DELETING A CHART

● If you need to delete a chart from your document, you can easily do this. User-defined charts can also be deleted easily.

● Click once on the chart to be deleted, so that there is a thin black line surrounding it.

● Click on the **Cut** icon on the Standard toolbar and your chart is deleted.

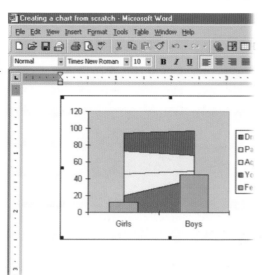

● Now go to the Edit menu in the toolbar and select **Cut** from the pull-down menu. The chart is now deleted from the document.

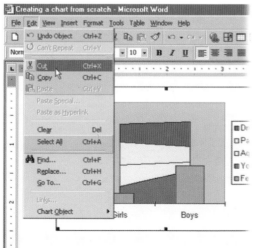

FORMATTING CHARTS

Using the formatting features of Word 2000, you can make any chart or graph look professional and give maximum visual impact to your data.

COLORS, BORDERS, AND BACKGROUNDS

This section of the book covers some of the main formatting features including customizing the border, adding colors, patterns, and backgrounds to charts, selecting gradients of color, and customizing the shading and texture.

1 SELECTING THE PLOT AREA

● If you saved the chart from page 58, open it to follow these steps. We'll alter the look of the chart by changing the Plot Area.

● Double-click on the chart and, if necessary, remove the datasheet from the screen.

● Move the mouse arrow over the main area of the chart until the **Plot Area** ScreenTip is displayed.

● Click once and the Plot Area is surrounded by a gray border showing that it has been selected.

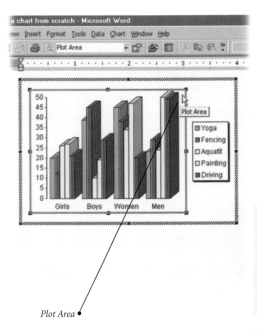

Plot Area ●

2 THE PLOT AREA DIALOG BOX

● Click on **Format** in the Menu bar and choose **Selected Plot Area** as the area to be formatted.

● The **Format Plot Area** dialog box opens with the **Patterns** tab at the top.

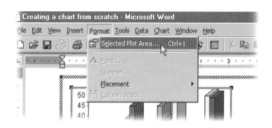

3 CUSTOMIZING THE BORDER

● To design your own border, begin by clicking on the **Custom** radio button.

● The first element of the border that can be decided on is the **Style**. Click on the down arrow to the right of the **Style** box to view a drop-down menu of the different styles of borders that are available. Select one by clicking on it.

● The **Sample** panel at the foot of the dialog box displays your selection.

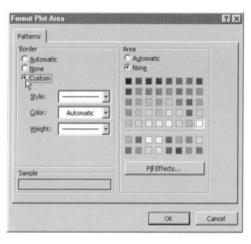

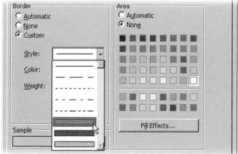

4 SELECTING THE COLOR

● The border can be given a color by first clicking on the arrow to the right of the **Color** box. A color palette drops down.

● A color is selected by clicking on it. Your choice appears in the **Color** box and as a border in the **Sample** box.

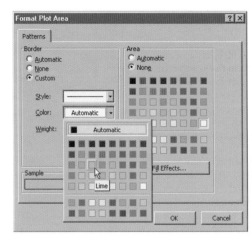

5 SELECTING THE WEIGHT

● The thickness of a border is known as its weight. Click on the down arrow to the right of the **Weight** box and select one of the options, which again is shown in the **Sample** box.

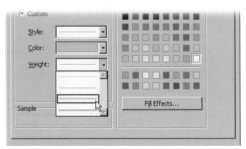

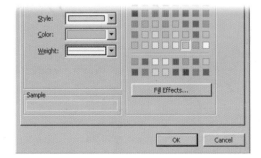

6 SELECTING A FILL AND AN EFFECT

● You can choose a solid-color fill by clicking on a color in the **Area** palette. Here we have selected one of the yellows.

● There also different background effects to choose from. Click on the **Fill Effects** button bar.

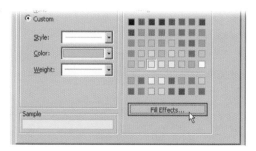

● The **Fill Effects** dialog box opens with four tabs along the top, each of which offers a selection of different effects. The **Gradient** tab is selected when you first open the dialog box.

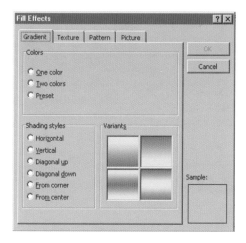

LAST CALL

It should be noted that it is always the last format choice that is applied to your chart. If you have made selections under the **Gradient** tab and then made further choices under the **Shading Style** tab, the **Shading Style** choices supersede the **Gradient** once you have clicked on OK. This is also true for any choices made under **Textures**, **Patterns**, or **Pictures**. You must have your chosen color format showing on the screen when you click on OK.

7 CUSTOMIZING THE GRADIENT

● If you click on **One Color**, and you have chosen a color previously, that color is displayed in the **Color 1** box.

● To change the color, click on the down arrow to the right of the **Color 1** box and the standard colors are displayed. You can choose a different color from here.

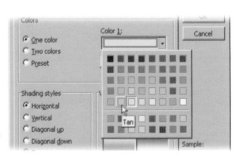

● To make the colors darker or lighter, drag the **Dark/Light** scroll bar to the right or left, or click on the **Dark** or **Light** arrows.

● If you click on **Two Colors**, you can choose a second color that will be combined with **Color 1**.

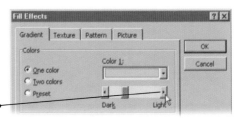

Lighten the color selection

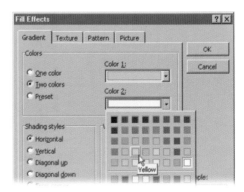

Choices recorded
If you choose a **Preset** design, and then click on the **One** or **Two Color** buttons, the choice you made under **Preset** is still available.

● If you click on **Preset**, you are given a large number of pre-designed color schemes that you may choose from for your chart. The Preset colors **Daybreak** are shown in the example.

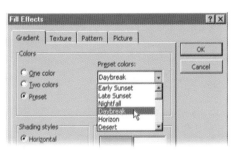

SELECTING A SHADING STYLE

● Click on each shading style in turn and the **Variants** preview panel displays your selection.
● As each one is chosen, it is displayed in the **Sample** box in the bottom right-hand corner of the window. In our example, we have chosen **From center**.

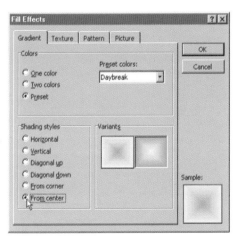

8 SELECTING A TEXTURE

● Click on the **Texture** tab at the top of the dialog box.
● Scroll up and down the texture choices to see the options that are available.

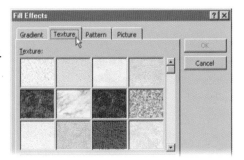

● The selection is shown in the **Sample** box at the bottom right-hand corner of the window.

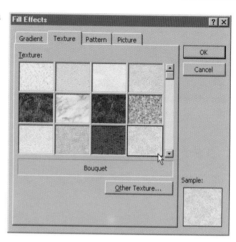

9 SELECTING A PATTERN

● Click on the **Pattern** tab at the top of the dialog box.
● Click on your preferred choice of pattern.
● The selection is again shown in the **Sample** box at the bottom right-hand corner of the dialog box.

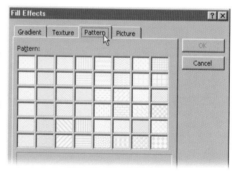

Selected pattern ●

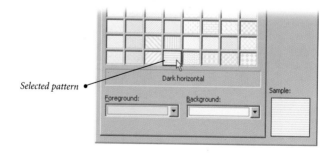

● When you have made your final choice, click on **OK** and you are returned to the **Format Plot Area** dialog box.

● The sample shown on the bottom left-hand side of the dialog box displays your final choice of border and fill effect.

● Click on **OK** to close the dialog box.

● Click off the chart to see the results of the color scheme you have chosen.

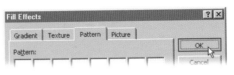

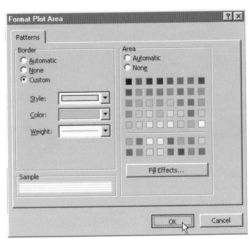

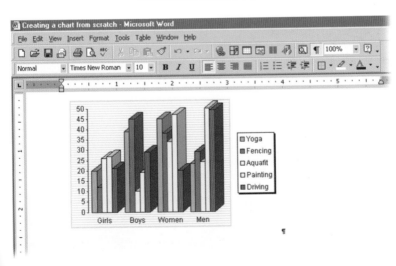

GLOSSARY

ALIGNMENT
In word-processing, this refers to the side of the text that is aligned in a straight vertical line along one side (for instance, left-aligned text is straight on the left side and the ends of the lines are ragged on the right).

AXIS
A line bordering one side of a chart showing incremental values or categories.

BLOCK (OF TEXT)
A selected portion of the text, highlighted in white letters on a black "block" on the screen.

BORDER
A decorative effect that can be applied to surround any amount of text that ends with a paragraph mark.

CELL
The smallest unit in a table, and the location for data.

CENTERED TEXT
One or more lines of text that are laid out on the page centered around the midpoint of the text area of a document.

COLUMN
A vertical line of cells extending from the top of the table to the bottom.

COPY
To copy a part (or the whole) of the text so that the same piece of text can be "pasted" into a new position (in the same document or another document) without removing the original piece of text.

CUT
To remove a block of text, in order to delete it permanently or to "paste" into a new position (in the same document or another document).

DATA SERIES
A group of related points in a chart, which are usually linked by belonging to the same category.

DATASHEET
A table that is always linked to a chart or a graph. Data represented in the chart or graph is entered, stored, and edited in the datasheet.

DIALOG BOX
A rectangle that appears on the screen and prompts you for a reply, usually with buttons, such as OK or Cancel.

FONT EFFECT
Effects that can be applied to areas of text, and that are in addition to the type of font and its size.

INDENT
The indent shifts part of the text or the whole graph across the screen.

INSERTION POINT
A blinking upright line on the screen. As you type, text appears at the insertion point.

PASTE
To insert text that has been cut or copied from elsewhere in the document, or from another document, at the present insertion point.

PLOT AREA
The area of a chart, usually in the center, where the data is calculated and laid out.

PRINT PREVIEW
A mock-up on the screen of exactly how your text will appear on paper. This allows you to make final changes to the look of your letter without wasting paper.

ROW
A horizontal line of cells extending from one edge of a table to the other.

RULER
Indicators at the top and left of the screen, with marks in inches or centimeters like a real ruler. Rulers also show the indents and margins of the text.

SCROLL
To scroll is to move up or down the document.

SCROLL BARS
Bars at the foot and the right of the screen that can be used to scroll around the document. The vertical scroll bar (on the right) is the more useful.

SHADING
Also known as a "Fill," this effect applies a background shade to an area of text or to a table.

X-AXIS
Usually the horizontal axis in a graph, which contains categories.

Y-AXIS
Usually the vertical axis in a graph, which contains values.

INDEX

ACKNOWLEDGMENTS

PUBLISHER'S ACKNOWLEDGMENTS
Dorling Kindersley would like to thank the following:
Paul Mattock of APM, Brighton, for commissioned photography.
Microsoft Corporation for permission to reproduce screens
from within Microsoft® Word 2000.

Every effort has been made to trace the copyright holders.
The publisher apologizes for any unintentional omissions and would be pleased,
in such cases, to place an acknowledgment in future editions of this book.

Microsoft® is a registered trademark of Microsoft Corporation
in the United States and/or other countries.